Peter Riley

HEATON HALL
and the Egerton Family

P & D Riley
in conjunction with
Manchester City Galleries

First published 2000
Reprinted 2002
Reprinted 2005
Reprinted 2007

P & D Riley
12 Bridgeway East,
Cheshire,
WA7 6LD

ISBN: 1 874712 45 X
ISBN: (From January 2007) 978 1 874712 45 9

British Library Cataloguing in Publication Data
A catalogue Record for this book is available from the British Library

Printed in England by JPS Design & Print, Leigh, Lancs

Introduction

THERE is something fascinating about old houses, particularly mansions which have been the home of the same family for generations, in some cases many centuries; and to look back on the events which have taken place in those country houses is to look back on the history of England itself.

This is particularly true of Heaton Hall, for it was the home of the influential Egerton family who owned large parcels of land as well as coal mining interests in North Manchester. Their interests stretched back to the 18th century, when the area around their estate, now known as Heaton Park, was farmlands which stretched as far as the moors and into the foothills of the Pennines.

The history of the Heaton family, with their lofty titles, is a reflection of bygone England and the hall's huge rooms, the servants and gardeners, the influential visitors to the hall - all added to the growing prestige of a family which was already held in high esteem by the hierarchy of this part of England. The family married into other landed gentry, strengthening a bond which, it appeared at the time, to be capable of ruling the nation for a thousand years.

Alas, times change and by the dawn of the 20th century the title remained (indeed as it does today), but Heaton Hall was no longer in the hands of the Egerton family. In 1901 the hall and park were sold to Manchester Corporation and thus ended almost 300 years of continuity at Heaton Hall. Today the treasures of the hall are enjoyed by more than 35,000 visitors a year, and it is hoped this modest book will help them enjoy their visit even more.

Peter Riley

Acknowledgments

The author and publishers would like to thank the following for their invaluable help in making this publication possible.

Ruth Greenbaum, *Manchester City Art Galleries Commercial Officer, for her constructive suggestions and enthusiasm for the project.*
Ruth Shrigley, *Curator of Heaton Hall, for meticulously checking historical facts and for offering invaluable advice throughout the preparation of the manuscript..*
Caroline Storey, *Curator of Decorative Arts, City of Manchester Art Galleries.*
Alan Seabright, *photographer, who took the modern photographs.*
The staff of Manchester Central Library Local Studies Department.

By the same author in this series:

Wythenshawe Hall and the Tatton Family (ISBN: 1 874712 39 5)   £3.

ONE

In the beginning

The Egertons were a family of considerable status under both the Plantagenet and the Tudor dynasties. The head of the family in King James I's time (1603-25) was Sir Rowland Egerton. He was made a baronet in 1617, and his wife was a daughter of Lord Grey de Wilton, thus helping to establish the first links in a chain which was to connect the two families and subsequently Heaton Hall and parklands for almost three centuries.

Sir Rowland's father, known by the unusual nickname of 'Black Sir John' had inherited an estate in Oulton, Cheshire, to which he later added further estates at Wrinehill, Staffordshire, and Farthinghoe in Northamptonshire, which he considered the most important possession. He died there in 1646 and Oulton was passed on to his second son while the Staffordshire and Northamptonshire estates were inherited by his eldest son.

In 1684 Sir John Egerton, the third baronet, married Elizabeth Holland, who was heiress to Heaton and Denton, her family having been lords of Denton, a parish to the east of Manchester, covering a massive 35,000 acres, which they had held since the 14th century.

Through natural inheritance the estate passed from father to son, but life was but a short span for many in those days, and it was Sir John's grandson, who himself was to die young at only 35 years old in 1756, who, according to historian H. Avray Tipping, M.A., F.S.A., made the decision to build a new hall on an elevated site in the Heaton estate, then a remote part of the country set among hills and country lanes.

But it was the 27 years old seventh baronet, Sir Thomas Egerton, who was to have the most impact on the future of Heaton Hall, for it was he who called on the services of one of England's most prestigious architects, James Wyatt, to transform the house. Wyatt had taken over the rein of favourite with the country's elite from Robert Adam who had himself made such a huge architectural impact throughout the mid 18th century. Wyatt, the sixth son of a Staffordshire timber merchant, came into his own in 1772 when his classical architecture was noticed by wealthy landowners and politicians, a recognition he was not slow to capitalise upon. In London he had designed, while still in his twenties, the Pantheon, a theatre and promenade, opened in January, 1772, which was patronised by the elite of the day.

Sir Thomas wanted Heaton Hall to be transformed from the style of the house owned by his father, and called for a greater magnificence in the building and grounds, similar in manner to the environments then being made fashionable by 'Capability' Brown, and Wyatt, to create an Italian villa in an English landscape.

In a book published in 1795 titled *A Description of the Country from Thirty to Forty Miles Round Manchester* by John Aiken, the author wrote:

"Heaton House, the seat of Lord Grey de Wilton, about four miles from Manchester, is beautifully situated on an eminence in a rich park, highly manured and well wooded.
"This truly elegant seat is built from a design of Wyatt. The centre is a circular projection with a dome at the top, that gives the whole a fine effect."

The importance of Heaton Hall at the time of Aiken's writings cannot be underestimated, for it was a very wealthy landholding, and records show that Sir Thomas Egerton's income from mining rights and land rents at that time were more than £5,000 per annum, a large amount

Sir Thomas Egerton,
1st Earl of Wilton

of money for that period. Records also show that as the century moved to a close the amount of income generated for the Egerton family increased dramatically, with the 1800 figure being recorded as £13,166, making it one of the richest and most influential families in Lancashire at that time. It is interesting to note that more than £2,000 of this income was coming to Sir Thomas from coal mining in nearby Radcliffe and Siddal Moor.

The huge income from these business interests was manifested at the start of the 19th century by the building of the park's Grand Lodge and the enclosure of the estate. By this time Sir Thomas Egerton had been elevated to the peerage with the title of Baron Grey de Wilton (in 1784) and in 1801 to first Earl of Wilton, a title taken from Wilton Castle in Herefordshire, which also had ancient links with the family.

There is no doubt that the first Earl of Wilton was a man of considerable foresight, for not only did his vision stretch far enough ahead to give him the confidence to bring in

Heaton Hall, the South Side

James Wyatt to restructure Heaton Hall, as we have seen; he also purchased many of its greatest paintings when he went on the Grand Tour of Europe with his wife and daughter in 1787-88. According to his own records he collected works by contemporary painters of the time, as well as copies of Old Masters in Italy. He also bought large quantities of furniture, clothing and porcelain in Paris and brought them back to Heaton Hall.

A lifelong music enthusiast, the Earl of Wilton played the cello and was an admirer of Handel, and the Heaton library held a large collection of music scores. He bought harpsichords for the use of his wife and children, and it comes as no surprise to learn that the hall's Music Room, with its superb organ built by Samuel Green, organ builder to George III, was an important part of family life.

Despite the successes he had with the rebuilding of Heaton Hall, the Earl of Wilton had great misfortune in his personal life, for of his six children he lost five through early deaths. The sole survivor was his daughter, Eleanor, who married Robert Grosvenor, First Marquess of Westminster. Because of the loss of his male heirs, the Earl's titles passed, on his death in 1814, by Royal Licence, to Eleanor's second son, Thomas Grosvenor, who took on the Egerton name and coat of arms in 1821 on his Coming of Age.

Also close by the hall is the circular Temple, (right) another 18th century addition to the grounds which was once used as an observatory by the Egerton family. In the late 1960s a balustrade which was constructed around the structure was removed.

TWO

A different lifestyle

In contrast to Sir Thomas, the first Earl, the Second Earl of Wilton conducted the affairs of Heaton Hall, in keeping with his more flambuoyant lifestyle. He was educated at Eton and Christ Church, Oxford, like so many of his contemporaries of the peerage, and following his education he married Lady Mary Stanley, the daughter of the 12th Earl of Derby by his second wife Eliza Farren, a famous actress.

It seems that Lady Egerton inherited some dramatic sense from her mother, for she happily entertained acting friends in the hall, and one, 'Fanny' Kemble, would astonish house guests during times she was appearing on stage in Manchester by coming down to dinner fully dressed for the part she was playing. One guest wrote of her entering the drawing room: "in full mediaeval costume of black satin and velvet.

Among the other guests who stayed at the hall were the Duke of Wellington, (who wrote more than 600 letters to Lady Wilton), William Huskisson, MP., (who is famous in history as the first person in the world to be killed by a train at Newton-le-Willows during the opening of the Liverpool to Manchester railway), and Disraeli, the future British Prime Minister.

It was recorded that the Earl was known to wear the ribbon of the Guelf Order in the hope that his contemporaries would think it was an Order of the Carter, an award only handed out to a notable few people as a personal award from the sovereign (which still applies today), and on one occasion the Earl was chosen to take an actual Garter award to Dresden to present to the King of Saxony and he wore it all the way to Germany "for practice!"

The rustic beauty of Heaton Hall pictured in 1832

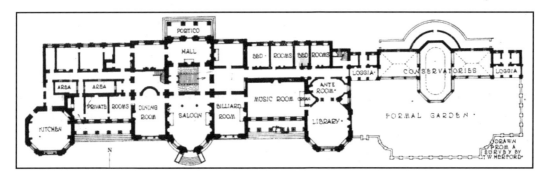

*Ground
Floor plan
of Heaton Hall*

In 1827 Lord Wilton established the Heaton Park races which were located where the boating lake is today. He was a keen sportsman and his passion for horses manifested itself in the popularity of his racecourse, though it seems if betting was allowed on the course by visitors it could soon deprive them of their cash, for the races became notorious for being fixed, or to put it in more diplomatic language for "the partiality of the judges." Crowds, too, soon got out of control and it wasn't long before respectable horse owners refused to take part in the Heaton Park races, thus ensuring its ultimate demise in 1839. A painting by F.C. Turner shows a meeting in 1835 which caused such controversy that two prize claimants Squire Osbaldeston and Lord George Bentinck fought a duel!

What life was like

But what was life really like at Heaton Hall in those far-off days? We imagine a life of luxury from the sheer size and magnificence of the house and parkland, and indeed it was if the notes of the actress 'Fanny' Kemble are to be believed. In 1830 she wrote Heaton Hall was "a charming specimen of a fine country house," and she was "engrossed by walking, riding, playing battledore and shuttlecock, singing and being exceedingly busy all day long about nothing. Heaton was looking lovely in all the beauty of its autumnal foliage lit by bright autumnal skies."

Her description of Lord Wilton is interesting, for it seems to sum up the man in an astute manner. 'Fanny' wrote: "He had an unusual taste for and knowledge of music; and had composed some that is not destitute of merit." She added that, "he was the beau-ideal of a dandy, with his slender, perfectly dressed figure, his pale complexion, regular features, fine eyes and dark glossy waves of hair, and the general aristocratic distinction of his whole person."

Of Lady Wilton, the actress once wrote that she was "strikingly handsome in person and extremely attractive in her manners. She was tall and graceful, and the upper part of her face, eyes, brow and forehead were radiant and sweet, and though the rest of her features were not radiantly beautiful, her countenance was noble and her smile had a peculiar charm of expression at once winning and mischievous."

These descriptions are fascinating because they offer us a vivid verbal picture of the two leading personalities of Heaton Hall, from a celebrated actress of the era. Lord and Lady Wilton both spent considerable time devoted to music, while Lady Wilton also concentrated on botany and embroidery, becoming a well liked figure and an authority on embroidery, writing *The Book of Costume* in 1847, having previously edited Stone's *Art of Needlework* in 1840.

Thomas Grosvenor Egerton, the second Earl, died in 1882 and in the years upto his death he had spent less time at Heaton Hall, following the death of his wife in 1858, having spent most of his time in London or Melton Mowbray. He tried to sell Heaton Hall and Park in 1866, but he was unsuccessful. A further attempt to sell was made in 1896, fourteen years after the Earl's death, but this too was unsuccessful.

Thomas' eldest son Arthur Edward Holland Grey, the third Earl, only survived his father by three years, dying in 1885, and his brother Seymour John Grey took on the mantle, becoming fourth Earl, before he too died in 1898.

It was Seymour's son, Arthur George, the fifth Earl, who was finally responsible for selling Heaton Hall and Park to Manchester Corporation in 1901 for the then princely sum of £230,000. Thus the connection of the Egerton's at Heaton Hall came to an end on March 14, 1902, when the formal agreement for the sale was completed.

Following the sale, the fifth Earl and his wife, the former Hon. Mariota Thellusson, left Heaton Hall. He survived until 1915. The lineage continued with their son Seymour Edward taking the rank of sixth Earl,

The North Front of Heaton Hall

and the line continued after Seymour's death in 1927 by Seymour William Arthur John Egerton, the seventh Earl, who was born on May 29, 1921 and died in 1999.

Heaton Hall from a contemporary sketch in 1795

Part of the magnificent Grand Staircase at Heaton Hall

THREE

Dawn of a new era

AS the 20th century dawned, Heaton Hall and its magnificent 600 acre park, were handed over to their new owners, Manchester Corporation. The transaction saw the end of an era for one of the North West's most historic families as the hall took on public ownership.

Shortly afterwards the park was placed under the jurisdiction of the Corporation's Parks Department, while in 1906 certain rooms in the hall were placed under the control of the Art Gallery Committee which wanted to use the house as a branch art gallery.

Complementing the outlook of Heaton Hall, though not as old as it looks, is the unusual Colonnade which used to be seen to great advantage from the house but is now almost invisible with the growth of trees. This unusual structure was once the front of the old Town Hall which stood in King Street, Manchester, until the present magnificent town hall opened in 1868.

In 1912, when the old Town Hall was demolished, the Corporation decided to have the facade preserved and rebuilt in Heaton Park, thus adding an extra dimension to the already superb parkland which, even today, comprises a large proportion, around 25 percent, of the green open space left in the Manchester conurbation.

It was decided to create a lake on the land once used as the race course, by damming a small stream to the south of the mansion, and this has proved a useful and popular asset to the park over the decades, and thousands of visitors have taken advantage of the lake for boating, fishing or merely feeding ducks since it became a public park.

The Colonnade from the lake

Inside the Hall

The number of rooms in Heaton Hall is considerable, although the number open to visitors these days is far fewer, but one can hardly expect the house to remain exactly as it was during the centuries of ownership by the Egerton family.

The West Wing which housed the kitchens and servants' quarters is in poor repair due to a disastrous fire and is not open to the public. However, the main rooms in the remainder of the hall have been restored so that visitors can gain some insight into how the Egerton's lived in Heaton Hall.

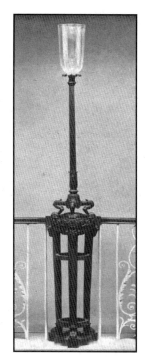

A Candle tripod on the staircase at Heaton Hall

The Corporation's purchase of the hall did not include the furniture, so the family sold the antiques separately. It was, in hindsight, a grave mistake, which left the newly purchased mansion looking forlorn and bare for some years. However, great effort has been made to purchase items to furnish the many very large rooms.

The first thing the visitor sees on entry from the North Side of the house is the Entrance Hall, a room with semi-circular ends, complete with niches and statues. The floor here is flagged, giving it an older appearance than the rooms which follow, and it is easy for the visitor to imagine days of yore when a butler would greet guests arriving at the house.

Moving from the Entrance Hall we next see the impressive Grand

Staircase which divides into two and turns back on itself until reaching the top floor. The staircase is complemented with French polished banisters and an ornate balustrade, tall candle tripods of cast iron with brass and lead decoration, and marble effect columns. It was a staircase definitely constructed to impress visitors of the Georgian and Victorian era, and the effect is still spectacular to this day.

The Saloon

In the central portion of Heaton Hall is the superb Saloon. The hugeness of this room is emphasised by its bay which once had a door leading out to the south front of the house, but which in recent years has been blocked in and windowed to complement the rest of the room.

The decorations and furnishings are a good example of the gracious style of living expected by the Egerton family. Two Georgian chimney pieces in the room also give us a clue to the problems of heating a room of this size.

Of the furniture in the Saloon the pink upholstered suite was originally made for Heveningham Hall, in Suffolk. Experts say the suite was probably made in the 1790s by a London cabinet worker and upholsterer named James Newton, and it is similar to a suite in Burghley House in Lincolnshire which was made by Newton's company. The upholstery itself, however, is thought to be Edwardian. There is no doubt that the suite fits in perfectly well in Heaton Hall and could have been made especially for this marvellous room.

The plasterwork in the Saloon is a work of art and was completed by Joseph Rose the Second, whose late 18th century workshop was in huge demand by stately homes throughout Britain at that period and he was paid £350 for his work in Heaton Hall. He was assisted by Giovanni Battista Maini who had also worked at Trafford Hall which was owned by relatives of Lady Wilton.

Over the chimney pieces there are oval plaster medallions which include the crest of the Egerton family, three crossed arrows. Also in the room can be seen sculptures which have stood in their present positions since the days of the fourth Earl of Wilton, at least four or five years before the hall was sold.

Above: Part of the Saloon at Heaton Hall showing a fireplace, statues and elegant plasterwork.

Right: The former entrance to the Saloon from the Central South Front.

The Dining Room

This is another splendid room which hasn't changed much in appearance in the past century, though, as mentioned earlier, the furniture in the room is not the original. The original dining chairs were supplied in 1775 by Gillow of Lancaster to Wyatt's pattern. History has now come back to life with the loan of mahogany dining chairs, designed by Wyatt, from Heveningham Hall in Suffolk.

A huge venetian window highlights this room in exactly the same way as it has for the past two centuries, the light reflecting on the mahogany chairs, the plaster frieze and wooden fire surround with its wonderful elaborate decoration of honeysuckle and beasts supporting an urn in the middle. The room also has a lovely apse in blue with three oval paintings with Bacchantes holding musical instruments in a predominance of blue, offering a truly classical look to this lovely room which also has a beautifully decorated plaster ceiling incorporating Greek shield motifs and four oval paintings depicting the four seasons.

A close up of the highly decorated Apse in the Heaton Hall Dining Room

The Dining Room and Apse in Heaton Hall as it looks today.

The Billiard Room

As expected from a room with this name, the first item which the visitor sees is a massive billiard table which dominates the space. This fifteen foot by eight foot table is believed to be an early 19th century model built by Gillow of Lancaster who supplied the original billiard table for Lord Wilton in 1771.

Heaton Hall was one of the first stately homes in Britain to have a billiard table as it became extremely fashionable to take up the sport in the 18th century. Having originated on the Continent, its early versions were played outdoors on grass, thus the reason why billiard table covers are still green baize!

It is an easy task to picture Lord Wilton and his friends around such a billiard table placing a wager on the outcome of a game.

The Billiard Room in Heaton Hall

The paintings on the walls remain the same as in the days of the Egerton family. They are large framed oil paintings on canvas by Michael Novosielski (1750-1795), a Polish artist. These nine paintings are the only surviving examples of Novosielski's work. Again we see the influence here of James Wyatt, for he brought the young artist to England to decorate the Pantheon in London. Novosielski later worked as a scene painter at the Haymarket's Theatre Royal and later still became an architect.

The nine paintings represent *Oeneus King of Calydon consecrating to Bacchus; Narcissus; Cymon and Iphegenia, daughter of King Oeneus; Orpheus the singer, son of the Muse Calliope; Meleager, son of King Oeneus, presenting the remains of the Calydonian Boar to Atlanta; Atlanta, daughter of Iasus, found on Mount Parthenius; Coronis, the Thessalian Princess; The Blind Belisarius and his Daughter;* and *The Family of Darius before Alexander.*

The Billiard Room is also furnished with a suite of six armchairs dating from 1790 with original silk upholstery, (which has now been covered to protect the fabric), a pair of mahogany fire screens dating from the 1780s, various 18th century vases and cut glass candelabra, as well as a couple of commodes of the period, and assorted items, all of which add to the atmosphere of the room.

The Music Room

It is almost certain this room was important to the Egerton family, particularly the first and second Lord Wilton, and undoubtedly played a major part in the life of the house, particularly when guests were staying at Heaton Hall. Completed by Samuel Wyatt, the elder brother of James, the room was inaugurated with music by Handel and Corelli on August 22, 1789., when Lord Wilton also played the cello to accompany a rendition of Corelli's 8th Concerto Grosso, and we can only imagine the wonderful day experienced by the gathering in the music room as the music filled the mansion and filtered across the splendid gardens.

Installed in 1790 the magnificent Samuel Green chamber organ with its subtle green, blue and gold colours still occupies the major part of one wall, reaching elegantly to the high ceiling. This long room is also furnished with a pair of Sheraton style satinwood veneer commodes dating from 1790, six chairs and a pair of sofas possibly by Chippendale the Younger dating from 1770, with original upholstery protected by loose covers, imitating the 18th century practice of covering upholstered furniture with 'case' coverings for everyday use. Of singular interest to visitors is the fact that the suite was once owned by the Duke of Wellington, whom, as we have seen, was particularly fond of writing to Lady Wilton.

The Music Room also houses a square piano made by Adam Benner of Soho, London, dating from 1779, a double action Grecian harp, circa 1824, and a harpsichord (the second most important piece of furniture after the organ).

H. Avray Tipping, MA., FSA., writing in 1925 commented on the Music Room: "The ceiling is of the coved type, which lent itself to much painted decoration, but this was probably never carried out. The room has a very interesting chimneypiece with bas-relief figures in the jambs and eagles above. This is in the side opposite to the windows, but the leading features occupy the centres of the ends.

"The one is a lofty and highly enriched doorcase framing the mahogany double doors. The other is an organ of similar proportions, but much greater size, for it reaches the full height of the walls. The panels below the pipes are painted in grisaille with appropriate subjects, the central one being winged maidens at an altar burning incense to the composer whose polychrome portrait appears in a ribboned medallion. A reference to the plan will show the ingenious manner in which the library and ante-room were shaped to give perfect completeness to themselves and at the same time a space for the organ."

The wonderful Samuel Green chamber organ in the Music Room

The Music Room at Heaton Hall as it looks today, complete with its
Samuel Green chamber organ, paintings, Grecian Harp and Harpsichord

The Library

Both the library and ante-library were remodelled in 1823 by Lewis Wyatt with mahogany bookcases which once contained an estimated 4,000 volumes, many of them on music, but these were removed after Manchester Corporation bought the hall at the beginning of the 20th century. However, since then, three of the bookcases have been reinstated in the ante-library.

These are 1824 mahogany veneer on a cedar and deal carcass made by Gillow of Lancaster. The ante-library also contains a selection of period furniture, including a patent 'metamorphic' chair, circa 1811, which converts into steps. To one side of the door is a fine portrait of Thomas Egerton, the second Lord Wilton, and on the other side is an intriguing painting of the Heaton Park races.

The Library Annexe
in Heaton Hall

The Cupola Room

Moving up the Grand Staircase to the first floor, the most ornate and unusual room in Heaton Hall is, without doubt, The Cupola Room, which dazzles the senses the moment you walk through the door. This large, round domed room was the private sitting room of the Dowager Lady Egerton, the mother of Lord Wilton.

The Cupola Room is in fact a rare survivor of rooms in the 'Etruscan' style which was in vogue for a short time in the late 18th century. The ornate walls and ceiling in the room were given over almost entirely to an Italian artist named Biagio Rebecca, a friend of Wyatt. Most of the room is decorated with oil-painted paper which has been pasted to the ceiling and walls, giving it its bizarre and ornate appearance.

The Cupola Room is sparsely furnished compared with other rooms, but does contain a suite of six chairs, two benches and two torcheres also painted in the 'Etruscan' style, and a large, ornate, chandelier hanging from the ceiling, the inner zone of which is made up of eight lozenges painted with the four elements of fire, water, earth and air; each element being painted in pairs. The outer zone of the ceiling includes ovals painted with figures of the virtues, including Temperance, Liberality, Fortitude, Meekness, Honour and Fame.

The walls are enhanced with semi-circular panels with a fan motif above. These eight panels depict gods and goddesses in triumph, including Diana, Venus, Juno, Mercury, Bacchus and Cupid. There are also a further twenty four panels in horizontal strips above the fan motifs, while over the fireplace is a painting titled *Sigismund weeping over the Ashes of Tancred*, which historians have described as possibly referring to Lady Egerton's widowhood because of its black background, though there is no actual evidence of this.

The Cupola Room and its ornate decoration

The Yellow Bedroom

This bedroom and the adjoining dressing room are important to the history of Heaton Hall because it is believed that these were the private rooms of Lady Eleanor Egerton. The rooms have recently been restored with a yellow and blue-green floral wallpaper, which is a reproduction of a wallpaper dating from the 1770s, discovered in a house in London which has been used as period paper in the absence of 'hard evidence' of the paper originally in these rooms. The dressing room would have been used extensively by Lady Eleanor for breakfast, writing and personal conversations. The bedroom itself is furnished with a selection of period pieces, including a four-poster bed designed by Wyatt for Heveningham Hall in Suffolk, dating from the late 18th century, and a lovely satinwood veneer screen with oval panels of interlaced cane also of the 18th century.

The Pink Bedroom

Across the landing from the Yellow Bedroom stands the Pink Bedroom and dressing room which have been decorated and furnished in the style fashionable in the period of the Second Lord and Lady Wilton. The paintings of ladies and children on the wall, and a print in the Dressing Room of Eliza Farren and a pastel portrait of Lady Egerton, later Countess of Wilton, reflect their artistic interest.

The bedroom also contains a collection of old books from the library of Winstanley Hall in Lancashire, an 18th century commode, various 18th century porcelain and a half-tester bed dating from the 19th century.

Indeed all the rooms contain too many items to include in this book, but each room offers visitors an information sheet with details of what is on display.

Finally

The history of Heaton Hall is not strictly confined to the Egerton family who lived there for so long, for in more recent years there have been events of historic importance taking place within the grounds which will be regarded by future historians as every bit as significant as the history of the family and the Hall

During the Second World War 133,516 aircrew cadets were stationed within the park en-route for flying training overseas, thus the park made a major contribution to the ultimate success of the conflict.

On May 31, 1982, thousands of people packed the park to witness the first ever papal visit to Britain when Pope John Paul II said Mass in the grounds, and consecrated priests into the Roman Catholic Church. A 10 foot high stone Papal Monument approximately 200 yards from the Colonnade and boating lake marks the spot.

Bibliography

Heaton Park, Manchester, by H. Avray Tipping, 1925. (Country Life Publications)

Heaton Hall, A guidebook published by Manchester City Art Galleries (now out of print)

Heaton Hall - An Illustrated Survey of the Lancashire Home of the Wilton Family (English Life Publications)

Heaton Hall, Manchester, Bi-centenary exhibition catalogue, 1972. (Manchester City Art Galleries)

Description of the Country from 30 to 40 miles around Manchester, by John Aiken, 1795.

Manchester Faces and Places, a series published from 1889 until 1914 (later titled *Lancashire Faces and Places*)

Debrett's People of Today, 1999.

Who's Who, 1999.

Pilgrimages to Old Homes, (Vol. 4), by Fletcher Moss (published by the author - 1909)

Photo Album

The Pink Bedroom

*Left: A glimpse of the tremendous
Cupola Room ceiling*

*Above: Fireplace and frieze
in the Cupola Room*

*Above: Part of the Colonnade
situated by the lake in Heaton Park*

Other titles in this series

Bramall Hall near Stockport was home to the influential Davenport family for centuries. The whole community of Bramhall Village grew up alongside the Lord of the Manor's estate and at one time the family held the power of life and death over the whole community. This book tells the story of the family and hall until the house was sold in the 19th century to the Nevill family. Bramall Hall eventually came into the posession of Stockport Council who still maintain this magnificent property.

Well illustrated with historic and modern photographs

Haigh Hall near Wigan, Lancashire, was owned for more than 600 years by the Bradshaigh family whose influence on the growth of industrial Wigan was second to none. The family was involved over the centuries in the Civil War, a crime of passion and several sordid affairs. In 1770 the Bradshaigh lineage came to an end at Haigh and the estate was inherited by the surviving daughter of the last Sir Roger Bradshaigh. This book tells the story from its early days until the present time.

Well illustrated with historic and modern photos.

Holmfirth in West Yorkshire has been a popular tourist attraction since the 1970s when BBC TV started filming *Last of the Summer Wine* here. But the town also has a long and fascinating history which encompasses everything from linen manufacturing to severe floods, that devastated the town, to being the centre of Britain's early film industry. It was also home to Bamforth's the company who made all those famous 'saucy' seaside postcards so beloved by the British! The text is complemented with a fine collection of photographs.

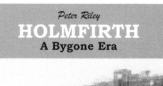

Any of the above titles can be ordered for only £3 each plus £1.00 postage & packing (UK only) direct from the publisher, or through any good bookstore